THE PERS

(NOTES, QUERIES AND OBSERV
WALLOON COLONIES AT SAN]
AND THORNEY, CA.

Seventeenth and Eighteenth Century Period

Introduced and compiled by

Trevor Bevis

COPYRIGHT :: 1992 :: TREVOR BEVIS
28 St. Peter's Road, March, Cambs. PE15 9NA
(Tel: (0354) 57286)

ISBN 0 901680 45 1

No part of this publication may be reproduced or transcribed in any form, by any means, electronic or mechanical, including photocopy, recording and information storage and retrieval system without first obtaining permission from the author.

Printed by Graytones Printers, Unit 17, King Street Industrial Estate, Langtoft, Peterborough PE6 9NF. Tel: (0778) 560261

Fenland view: two-hundred and fifty years ago

THE PERSECUTED

(NOTES, QUERIES AND OBSERVATIONS OF
HUGUENOT AND WALLOON COLONIES AT SANDTOFT AND
HATFIELD CHASE, SOUTH YORKSHIRE AND THORNEY,
CAMBRIDGESHIRE)

Seventeenth and Eighteenth Century Period

Introduction

TRACING family roots is a time consuming if fascinating and popular pastime. Rooting out the past relative to ancestry demands a high degree of patience and is sometimes attended by frustration and disappointment as well as delight and a sense of achievement. A few years ago I prepared and published an account of the Thorney colony and its offshoots, gatherings of Huguenot and Walloon families that had settled in the Cambridgeshire Fens about the middle of the seventeenth century. Then I realised that a great deal more information was to hand, far more than my book "Strangers in the Fens" could economically accommodate. Indeed, to seek a conclusion to such an absorbing subject would be quite impossible, especially as regards the numerous surnames, each deserving of individual research.

The establishment of the colony at Thorney within the ancient constituency of the Isle of Ely owed its existence to the much troubled colony at Sandtoft, near Hatfield in Yorkshire. It largely came about from the unfortunate and traumatic persecution of those settlers resident at Sandtoft and Hatfield Chase who already bore the memories of persecution of themselves, their parents and ancestors subjected to the worst kind of persecution in their homelands beyond the English Channel. The English commoners living in the Hatfield area, fearful of loss of livelihood as their fens were drained, rose vehemently against them time and time again and this encouraged the refugees to trek southwards and settle in the area around Thorney.

Towards the end of the nineteenth century and within the first decade of the twentieth century, certain individuals with access to various documents made notes and observations outlining the work and movement of the colonists. These first appeared in successive editions of Fenland Notes and Queries, edited by W. H. Bernard Saunders, F.H. Hist. Soc., and Rev. W. D. Sweeting, M.A., between 1889 and 1909.

The accummulation of notes give an enlightening glimpse into a subject unique in many ways. Normally, French speaking refugees usually described as Huguenots or Walloons depending on the geographical situation of their respective native lands, were largely associated with the cloth trade and it was with that particular enterprise that the colonies at London, Canterbury, Norwich and other places were famously and closely associated.

The refugee families at Hatfield Chase and subsequently at Thorney had little if no connection with weaving but were primarily concerned with land drainage and agriculture. The Flemish in particular and the Dutch excelled in land drainage and while in England were supervised by that renowned land drainage engineer and countryman, Sir Cornelius Veymuyden. Despite some errors of judgement this man had put his hand to the mammoth, mind boggling undertaking to drain the Cambridgeshire Fens, an area of far greater acreage than that at Hatfield where he had also been involved.

It is hoped that the notes and observations reproduced in this booklet will be of some use to those that are desirous of tracing their ancestry. Certainly it will offer indisputable proof of the links between Sandtoft and Thorney and allow greater convenience for those interested in delving into the vision, work, disappointment, anguish and achievement of those dedicated, talented souls who created prolific soil from the dreary wastes of fen.

TREVOR BEVIS, 1992.

28 St. Peter's Road,
March, Cambridgeshire,
PE15 9NA.

STOVIN'S MANUSCRIPT

At the King's initiative Sir Cornelius Vermuyden and other Gentlemen Participants seized the opportunity to reclaim 70,000 acres of waste fen between Doncaster and Hatfield, described as a den of waters fed principally by the rivers Trent, Torn, Went and Dunn with the great river Humber to the north. For the ease of his tenants, King Charles contracted Veymuyden who is better known for his scheme to drain the Cambridgeshire Fens, to rid the fen around Hatfield of its water and affect a satisfactory scheme to enable the tenants and other of his subjects to pursue a satisfactory and productive existence on land which had been previously ruined by regular inflow of those rivers.

Stovin's manuscript of 1752 outlines the scheme which was beset with problems and aggravated by riotous action against the Participants and their workers of foreign extraction. Many of the Participants originated from Continental countries and the settlers, ordinary families that had suffered persecution for their faith, were attracted to the scene by the promise of continuous and profitable production.

The sum of £300,000 was expended on work to drain Hatfield fens and the King sold his manor there to Vermuyden. Other notable people benefitted too, but the common residents viewed the scheme as a threat to their right of livelihood, principally centred on wild fowling and fishing. In an endeavour to placate the commoners it was ordered that the Participants should contribute £400 towards employing the natives in the manufacture of sack-cloth, etc.

At the outset of the scheme, according to Stovin a large number of Dutch and French Protestants, refugees from persecution rife on the Continent, came to settle in the vicinity of Hatfield and they brought with them their own minister who addressed them in two languages. At the outbreak of the Civil War in 1643 the commoners of Epworth and Mysterton took up arms against the King and, assisted by Parliamentary soldiers, tore up fences and entered the enclosed lands, setting fire to the settlers' houses and crops to the loss and damage of £20,000. In their rage they defiled Sandtoft church and buried carrion beneath the communion table, stripped lead from the roof and carried away the seats.

Arms were brought to bear against the rioters and eventually they were suppressed. But several of the families had grown weary of the dangers and hardships and broke away from the colony, pursuing interests in other directions, notably at Thorney, an island in the Cambridgeshire Fens where they were welcomed by the Earl of Bedford, owner of a large estate, much of it drowned land. It is conceivable that Vermuyden who had accepted a contract to drain the Cambridgeshire Fens, encouraged the Sandtoft settlers to move to that area.

To maintain the level around Hatfield in some degree of order and stability was a costly operation. The threat of hostility did not end and the Commissioners worked continually in fear of the commoners. Legal recourse was commenced in an attempt to satisfy the natives by letting them have more common land but they still demanded more and threatened civil disorder as previously.

The Commissioners prevailed upon Nathaniel Reading, a strong principled and respected owner of land in Hatfield Level to take a stance against the commoners and with the blessing of the House of Lords he hired men and arms, beginning his action in September 1655. The rioters were finally quelled after thirty-one battles which resulted in several of Reading's men being killed and wounded. The church at Sandtoft was then repaired and the congregation restored. Eventually it was deemed that Hatfield Level was at last safe and it began to flourish.

Stovin wrote that a few quiet years elapsed and the battle enjoined in a legal manner. In 1691 the commoners' demands were presented to the Exchequer and various acreages were set out for the use of the commoners of Epworth and Mysterton. In addition several thousand acres were made over at Epworth South Moor and Butterwick Moor "free from interruption of the Participants and freed and discharged from all drains, bridges or any part of the Fen Farm Rent or Sewer Rates". Thus was it implied that all differences would be resolved.

That was not to be the case. The commoners reacted negatively and were in fact anxious that the Participants remove themselves from the Level altogether. A large number of men, women and children led by a Mrs. Popperwell, wife of a lawyer of doubtful reputation, bore down upon the fences and demolished and burnt them. They then destroyed the corn and laid open productive land as common. The resilient owner, Mr. Reading, urgently turned to the Participants who owed him £3,000 but they alleged that they had no money, the rioters having laid waste their lands, too. However, the Participants offered their lands in Epworth manor to Mr. Reading for six years and granted him over and above the normal rate. Fully aware of the risks he reluctantly accepted.

The owner had enclosed his land with several miles of fences and sown more than a thousand acres of rape and corn. He met the commoners for consultation but they rejected all reason and seized the opportunity to amass in formidable numbers. The rioters attacked Mr. Reading, "his sons and servants night and day and often shot at them (and) they killed his cattle and fired his house at night with a desire to burn him, his wife and family in their beds".

Afterwards, in great numbers having disguised themselves and carrying weapons, the rioters destroyed all adjacent buildings and took axes to Mr. Reading's orchards, cutting down the trees. They broke into a new house he had been obliged to build for himself and his family, stole his goods and set fire to fences, then drove his cattle into the corn fields. The military intervened and many of the rioters were committed to Lincoln Assizes and sent to prison. Others were outlawed. The action did, at least, subdue the commoners who abandoned violent acts in favour of legal representation and, through the services of their solicitor, Mr. Popperwell, they continued verbal abusement and to defy Parliament.

Stovin's account of the dispute includes the surnames of refugees that had settled in the vicinity of Hatfield. These are given as were spelt in 1752. Several names which he listed are identical with names recorded in the French Register at Thorney but it should be borne in mind that the spelling sometimes varies.

Dublieque	Renault	Le Coup	Delagay
Turgoin	Renard	Le Talle	Le Hair
Blancart	Frank	Lenards	Dewitt
Bonuel	Vanplue	Dubois	Licuq
Siaufair	Tuysen	De la Priam	Amory
Longue	Beharch	Smaque	Tuffin
Delahay	Stirpin	Cony	Egard
Vanderbee	Hernu	Caidoy	Le Flour
Hahear	Lilouq	Descamps	Blancar
Pinsoy	Librand	Coquelar	Lespier
Dubertlet	Baurudit	Leliew	Le Roy
Brungue	Dilanoy	Le Grand	Rammery
Acfair	Dumoulin	Breche	Pinstoy
Morvillion	Icmemime	Delespaer	Rabau
Flahon	Henegrave	Duverlier	Vienin
Beamarch	Senoir	Clebaux	Derique
	Chauval	Le Roux	

Names of the Gentlemen Participants and others at Hatfield Level:

Lucious Vanvolkenbourgh, Cornelius Vanbueren, Samuel Vawpeener, Marcus Vanvolkenbourgh, Jn. Vanbaerle, Wm. Vanweely, Philip Jacobson, Isaac Vanpeener, Picter Vanpeener, Picter Cryspenick, Widow of Edward Bushope, Marceillus Vandareen, Dirique Semey, Leonard Catts, Fabrian Ullict, Riolf Franken, Sebastian Franken, Widow of Michael Croystyn, Sir Philip Vernatti, Abraham Dolens, Dionisius Vandrace, Charles de Bruxelles, Woulter de Gelder, Jn. Vandimer, Sir James Catts, Abraham Strys, Jacob Strys, Raynier Curnelison, The Professor Goce, Jacob Droogbroot.

These gentlemen held parts of 24,505 acres of the Level. King Charles the First possessed 24,505 acres and the commoners of those parts, being a great many, shared a similar number of acres. Total acreage: 73,515.

Five ministers officiated at Sandtoft church – Monsr. Berchett, Monsr. Deekeshuel, Monsr. Delaprix, Monsr. Delaporte and Monsr. Lavenely. After the church had been destroyed by the rioters the site was regarded as common. According to Stovin many of the first colonists were buried there and the register which by great fortune accidently came into Stovin's hands (but has since been lost) included the name of Monsr. Berchett's wife.

Le 26 May 1651. Dam Katherine Lecoq de la Femme de Monsr. Berchet Ministre, Enter a Sandtoft.

Several hundred children were baptised at Sandtoft church and there were numerous marriages. Women always retained their maiden names. (See Stovin's selection of names from the missing register of marriages, baptisms and burials on another page).

The vicious onslaught of the commoners was responsible for many of the refugees leaving the area for other places where they were generally sympathetically received. Several families trekked 75 miles south to the Cambridgeshire Fens by invitation of the Earl of Bedford and established roots at Whittlesey and Thorney where they were able to pursue similar occupations and assemble unmolested in the remains of Thorney abbey.

* * * * * * *

REGISTER OF THE FRENCH CHURCH AT THORNEY CAMBRIDGESHIRE

A book entitled as above was transcribed and edited by Mr. Henry Peet, F.S.A. in 1903. It contains 1,717 baptismal entries beginning February 11 1654 and ending October 3 1727 by which time the colony had practically ceased to exist, many of its members pursuing their crafts and professions in other places and being anglicised through marriages. Not unnaturally a large number of names have, over the centuries, become corrupted usually through the signing of deeds and written incorrectly into church registers. Some are beyond recognition. Happily many of the Sandtoft/Thorney names still persist in the Fenland.

Owing to profound religious intoleration there were two major immigrations of Huguenots and Flemish Walloons from France and Flanders respectively. The first commenced a few years anterior to the massacre on St. Bartholomew's Day in 1572 when thousands of men, women and children were killed and others imprisoned. The persecution continued at verious levels of intensity for several years and many families emigrated to England, setting up colonies initially at Canterbury and Southampton. The second major emigration, far greater, occurred at the Revocation of the Edict of Nantes in 1685 which effectively removed guarantees of safety for French Protestants in their homeland. Few if any of this wave of immigrants settled at Thorney. To some extent Sandtoft and Thorney colonies comprised of families and individuals descended from parents and grandparents who had arrived in England during the earlier period with additional arrivals in the first half of the seventeenth century.

    Mr. Peet was in no doubt that many of the colonists at Thorney had been forced to leave the Hatfield Level. Reclamation of the Fen around Hatfield began in 1626 and two years later eighty families from Walloon Flanders settled there. More immigrants joined them in 1635 from Normandy and the Walloon country.

    The problems that beset Hatfield Fens lasted for 25 years during which time the church at Sandtoft and the village were virtually destroyed. The French-speaking congregation at Thorney officially settled there in 1652, but one or two families of foreign extraction had been observed living there in the 1640's. Gregory Leti, Italian historian wrote in 1683 that many of Thorney's original settlers were then still living and could confirm his record of events in which he stated that some Frenchmen near Doncaster who had been molested by peasants enquired of the Earl of Bedford if they could rent the waste area of his estate near Thorney and drain it and cultivate it. The far-sighted nobleman, grateful of the offer, made honourable conditions with the Frenchmen who with great toil and admirable fortitude drained the entire estate of about 17,000 acres. Initially 56 families of the colony received permission to meet for worship at Thorney abbey.

8

The colonists at Thorney were not without problems, Fenmen displaying varying degrees of hostility for the same reasons argued by the commoners of Hatfield Level. Due to the large area involved concerted action in the Cambridgeshire Fens was not possible and despite the odd instances of blowing up a sluice and breaching river banks little more transpired of a serious nature. (Read "Strangers in the Fens" (T. Bevis) - a brief history of the colony at Thorney and off-shoots at Parson's Drove and Guyhirn).

The founding members of the Thorney colony were: Thomas Benitland, Anthony Blancart, Peter Descamps, Peter Egar, James Flahau, Simon le Haire, George Hardick, Josias Harley, Peter de la Haye, Jean de Lannoy, Isaac de Lanoy, Joel de Lespierre, Anthony Massingarbe, Peter du Quenne and Hosea Tafin (15).

Surnames of 22 families that followed: Amory, Beharelle, Blique, du Bois, Clais, le Conte, Coquelar, Desbiens, Desquien, le Flour, Fontaine, Frochart, Gouy, Hancar, le Leu, Marquilier, Rennard, Ramery, le Roux, le Roy, le Talle, Vennin.

The Thorney colony continued to grow and other surnames added during its early existence, were: Becue, Caillet, Castell, Descou, Foster, Hennoc, Hernu, le Houcq, le Grand, Manie, Morillon, Pinchon, Smaque, Vermeil, du Verlier and Wantier. Another refugee associated with the Cambridge-shire Fens, John Cuuelie, an ancestor on the maternal side of the writer, had added his signature to several others that petitioned Oliver Cromwell to save them from the fury of the Hatfield Level rioters.

Further evidence as to the origin of several alien names recorded in Sandtoft Register and the baptismal register at Thorney is given by Mr. Francis Bayley, F.S.A., author of "Bailleuls of Flanders and Bayleys of Willow Hall" (Thorney), 1900. In it he wrote that he had ascertained as far as possible that most of the settlers at Thorney could be traced to Flanders, Artois and the Pays Conquis. Almost every surname in Thorney French register is traceable in the register of the church of St. Guisnes.

QUERIES AND OBSERVATIONS

The following notes, queries and observations transpired after a question appeared in "Fenland Notes and Queries," a series of quarterly magazines published between 1889 and 1907. The enquirer signing himself "S.E." referred to a Mr. Warner, author, who had written: "Nothing appears to be known for certain of the continental origins of this (Thorney) community."

"S.E." had perused a transcript of the registers (1668-1685) of the Protestant Church at Guisnes and discovered that it contained a great number of the names which he had previously seen in extracts from the Sandtoft and Thorney French registers.

That at Sandtoft was said to have been carefully kept from 1641 to 1682 and the register at Thorney was used between 1654 and 1727. The conclusion was that these two congregations were connected and that the districts east of Calais and Dunkirk of which the churches of Marck and Guisnes, six miles east of Calais were the centres, was the source from which many families had sought refuge in England, eventually settling near Sandtoft and later at Thorney. The first minister of the colony at Thorney, Ezekiel Dannois (1652-1674) was identified by M. V. J. Vaillant as being the same minister of the Huguenot congregation at Boulogne (1638-1650).

The query inspired much interest and many contributions by various correspondents appeared in successive publications of Fenland Notes and Queries. In the author's opinion they are of considerable importance in a collective sense to any that are desirous of learning more about the colonies at Sandtoft and Thorney, and especially to those who are desirous of tracing continental ancestry over a period of four centuries of Dutch, French and Flemish association.

The notes, queries and observations will be found on the following pages of this booklet.

31.—**The French Colony at Thorney.**—(No. 25).—The date of the licence to Stephen de Cursol to preach at Thorney is said to be 1600. There was not a French Congregation at Thorney at that date. The Survey of Thorney, quoted by Warner, would probably be made in 1594. The Manor was in possession of the Crown in 1596. In 1605 the first Drainage Bill was rejected by Parliament on the third reading–quoting a treatise written in 1629–"At Thorney Abbey my Lord of Bedford lets between 300 and 400 acres of rising ground upon which the abbey stands, for £300 per annum, whereas the rest of the Lordship of Thorney, containing 16,000 or 17,000 acres of drowned ground is estimated as it now lieth of little or no value." In 1630 the Drainage Works commenced under the Earl of Bedford and 13 gentlemen adventurers. Vermuyden was afterwards introduced into the Bedford Level. He had previously in November 1628 made a contract of the drainage of certain lands in the Isle of Axholme. He and his co-adventurers the Participants, brought over Dutch, Walloons and French from Normandy and other parts of France who stipulated for certain rights which were readily granted. Among these was the right to worship according to the dictates of their conscience. They founded congregations and had pastors to preach to them in their own tongue*. Of this congregation there is a precious relic preserved at Thorney, a French Register of Baptisms during 1654-1727, a small folio containing 1,710 entries.

We may note on the appointment of "de Cursoll" by Bishop Wren, that Warner gives in the first edition of his History of Thorney 1640 as the date which I should say is nearer the mark. We find persons of the same name prominent members of the two congregations of Sandtoft and Thorney. David le Conte represented Sandtoft at the Coloque in London. The same name afterwards occurs as the Thorney representative. It is fair to assume that the congregation at Sandtoft was formed prior to that of Thorney.

It appears that Peter Bontemps was the first Pastor at Santoft. He was brought over by the Participants (most probably with the approbation of the Bishop of the Diocese). In June, 1636, he writes: "I have dwelt here nearly two years, during which time the number of strangers in this place has increased by more than one-half, and is still daily increasing." He asks, If a Church for the French congregation is not to be built and maintained? that he may be dismissed? He left in August, 1636. He practised the Geneva discipline in all things by Deacons and Elders. According to *Dr. Farmerie*, the Chancellor, in his letter to the Bishop, who, after the congregation had been without a Minister for the space of two years, 1638, sent down among them *Dr. Cursol*, "who had taken the Oaths of Allegiance Supremaice and Canonical obeidiency to your Grace." *Lauds* reign of persecution was shewing signs of coming to an end early in 1640. Before the year was out we hear of a petition, "To the House of Lords, on behalf of the French, and Dutch congregation assembled in the Isle of Axholme, for redress against the above-quoted Dr. Farmery, complaining that they did not enjoy the free exercise of their religion, *as it was in those parts reformed from whence they came;*" and that he further thrust upon them one "Cursoll," a *Franciscan friar*. Such being their opinions of the man, it need not be a matter of surprise that he was not recognised and never officiated at Thorney. In evidence he was spoken of very disrespectfully. M. Dispaigne was heard to say, that M. de Cursoll was a thief, that he had stolen from the people of his Church £30 sterling, that he was a very bad and dishonest man.

In 1643 we hear of John d' Espaigne, a minister of the French Church at Santoft, and Stephen Cursoll who likewise pretends himself to be a minister for private ends, and by respects endeavouring to disturb the peace and quiet of the French congregation in London. Such was Cursoll from what we gather, and his appointment to Thorney by Wren could not be earlier than 1640, from the best evidence we can command.

S. E.

* They were not poor illiterate men, to be compared with our navvies of the present day. They were, from all we gather, steady, upright people, men of education and abilities. In 1656 they appealed to Cromwell for protection. Of the 54 persons who signed the petition, only three signed by *mark*. In this they compare very favourably with a Grand Jury at Wisbech within the memory of the writer, one of whom signed with a cross.

652.—Santoft Register.—Much enquiry has been made from time to time for the original registers of this church, but without success. Hunter, in his *South Yorkshire*, 1828, gives a list of names of the foreign settlers on the Levels.

The following extracts from the Santoft French Register, given by Stovin in his MS. notes, may be of interest to many persons in the Fenland, especially those who are descended from members of the French congregation settled at Thorney or in the neighbourhood. These settlers are referred to in 1683 by Gregorio Leti, the Italian historian, as having been driven from near Doncaster by the turbulence of the peasantry.* Some 40 years before he wrote, Smiles says that out of 71 families settled at Santoft, 14 removed to Thorney. Again we are told that there were at one time 200 families settled at Santoft, numbering upwards of 1,000 souls, of whom more than 50 moved southwards to Thorney.

The desperate resistance of those besieged in Rochelle, in 1627, rendered a residence in French Flanders so insecure and uncomfortable, that about 80 families fled to England from the neighbourhood of Ypres and Calais, and settled in the vicinity of Doncaster, near Hatfield Chase, in 1628–9. Among these were de la Prymes, from Ypres, one of whose descendants lived in Postland, near Crowland.*

George Stovin, the author of the MS. above referred to, was born 1695-6, and lived in the Levels in the vicinity of Crowle. He is said scarcely to have left the district, and he was buried at Winterton in 1780. This MS. has been repeatedly quoted by Hunter, Stonehouse, Peck, Wainright, Read, &c. It was found in 1880 among some books in the office of a solicitor at Doncaster; whence it came, and how long it had been lying there, could not be explained. Having now been communicated to the Yorkshire Society, all risk of its loss is removed.

Mr. Stovin's writing not being so clear in some cases as could be wished, it is possible, and more than probable, that some of the names, &c., in the extracts here given, may not be perfectly correct. The same remarks might apply to most other transcripts.

S. EGAR.

---

* Hug. Soc. ii, 330.

* See Pryme's Diary, pa e 266. Surtees Soc. Pub. vol. 54.

Part of the Register of the French Protestants' Church at Sandtoft.

1643   Le 3rd jour d Avril, 1643, Mart Dubliq et Eñz. Teurqoin ont este Espouzez danse L Eglise de Santoft.
      Le 11th Juni, 1643, Anthoine Blancart et Marie Bondvel ont este Espouzez a Sandtoft.
      Le 22d October, 1643, Anthoine Scanfaire et Jenne Longuespee ont este Espouzez a Santoft.
      Le 5 Novembr., 1643, Pier Delahaye et Jenne Henegrave ont este Espouzez a Santoft.
      Le 28 Jan. 1648 (? 1643), Noe Ager et Jeann Caidoy ont este Espouzez a Sandtoft.

1644   Le 19 Maii, Jesay Beamarm et Susann Lehouq ont este Espouzez a Sandtoft.
      Le 14 Jullii, Jaques Pinssoy et Susann Leespier ont este Espouzez a Sandtoft.
      Le 10 June, Jehan Leleu et Judith Lenoy ont este Espouzez a Sandtoft.
      Le 21 Julii, Jaques Leroy et Maria Pinsfoy ont este Espouzez a Santoft.

1645   Le 15 July, 1645, Simon Acfair et Maria Le Roy ont este Espouzez a Santoft.
      Le 3d Augt. Francois Derick et Cath. Delespiser ont este Espouzez a Santoft.
      Le 10 Augt. Anthoine Leflour et Marie Renault ont este Espouzez a Santoft.

1646   Le 30 Mars, Pier Amory et Maria Watson ont este Espouzez a Santoft.
      Le 2 Aug. Jacob Renard et Maria Frank ont este Espouzez a Santoft.

1647

1648   Le 29 Oct. Christian Smaque et MagDelein Descamps ont este Espouzez a Santoft.
      Le 14 Jan. Michell Lebrand et Ester Pensoy ont este Espouzez a Santoft.
      Le . . . Jan. Piere Descamps et Ester Cony ont este Espouzez a Santoft.

1649   Le 1 Julliet, Isaac Delanoy et Marie Du Battelet ont este Espouzez a Santoft.
      Le 15 Julliet, Jaques Harnew et Jenne Le Roy ont este Espouzez a Santoft.

1650   Le 3 Juin ont este Espouzez Oser Legrand et Jenne Hancar, a Santoft.
      Le 1 de Jan. Jaq. Dumoulin et Cath Legrain ont este Espouzez a Santoft.

1651   Le 23 Avril, Anthoine Blancar et Marie Lespiere ont este Espouzez a Santoft.

1652   Le 9 Nov. ont este Espouzez Jaques Coquelar et Ester Morilion a Santoft.

1665   Le 15 Febier, Abram Egard et Jeanne Delaynoy ont este Espouzez a Santoft.
      Le 25 Julliet, David Morrillion et Catherin Banruedt Espouzez a Santoft.
      Le 30 Octr. ont este Espouzez Piere Lelieu et Ester Lenoir.
      Le 1 Nov. ont este Espouzez Isaac de bacy et Eliz. Amory.
      Le 18 Jan. ont este Espouzez Iscnbar Chavatte et Ann Morrillion.
      Le 18 Jan. ont este Espouzez Marc de coup et Marie Morrillion.
      Le 8 Fevrier, ont este Espouzez Isaac Vanplue et Jeann duvertier.
      Le 14 Mar. ont este Espouzez Jacob Tissen et Marie Baurudet.

1666   Le 28 Nov. ont este Espouzez Isaac Beharelle et Jean Discamps.
      Le 23 Jan. ont este Espouzez Jacob Tyssen et Sara de Raedt.
      Le 23 Jan. ont este Espouzez David Letalle et Maria Amory.
      Le 13 Feb. ont este Espouzez Piere Tyssen et Eliz. Leenards.

1667 Le 24 Feb. ont este Espouser Abram Beharelle et Elizabeth Letalle.
Le 26 Feb. ont este Espouser Piere Leleu et Maria duvertier.
Le 4 Mars, ont este Espouser Isenbar Chavatte et Maria Smaque.
1670 Le 4 d Avril sont Maries Abram Bareel* et Francoise Sterpin; Matthias Priem et Sarah Smaque.
1671 Le 25 d Janivar ont este Maries Isaac Desbiens et Joanna Waterloo.

Baptise à Santoft.

1642 Le 19 May a este Baptissee Eliz. fille de Noe et de Marguerit Guiselin p' pise de Crowle.
Le 22 Febrier a este Baptize Isaac fils de Jean Beharrelle et de Jane Jordain.
Le 26 Feb. a este Baptize Jacob fils de Matt^w. Porree et de Maria Jaquemine.
Le 26 Feb. a este Baptize Susann fille de Osee Tafin et de Sara de Zomber.
Le 26 Mar. a este Baptize Michael fils de Custaw Legrand et Magelen Chavatte.

1643 Le 3 Ap^l. a este Baptize Pierre fils de David Morrillion et Anne Letalle.
Le 23 d Jullet a este Baptize Jaques fil de Jehan Le Talle et Judith Descamps.
Le 23 Jullet a este Baptize Jean Hernu fil de Jaques et Jenne Lombard.
Le 24 Sept. a este Baptize Matthew Prime fil d Crullin et de Sara Bresmr.
Oct. 25, Marg^t. Brungne fille de Matthew et de Marguerit Bale, a este Baptise.
Nov. 26, Jaques fills Jehan Letalle et de Jaquenime Tissen a este Baptise.
Dec. 3, Isaac fills de Jaques Flahau et de Jeanne Chatelet a este Baptise a Sandtoft, Les Testimoys sont Isaac Amory et Judith Leflour.
Dec. 5th. Ester Vienin fill de Jaq. Vienin et Judith Dubois a este Baptise.
Marc 14, Marie Amory fil de Isaac et de Maria Morillion bapt.

1643 Le 22 Jan. Pier Berchet fil de Monsr. Berchett, minister, de Santoft, Bapt.
Susan fill de Anthonine Dubois et Susanna Morillion, Bapt.

1644 Issenbar fils de Isenbar Chavatte, Bapt.
Le 1 Sept. Susan fil Roland Dubois et Magdalen Cardue a Baptise.
D^o. Matthias fils de Charles Prime et Pree Messman a Baptise.
Piere fills de Jean et de Jennine Morillion a Baptise a Santoft.
Ann fill David Morrillion et Ann Letalle.
Jacob fill de Isaac Vennin et Cath. Smaque, Bapt.
Jacob fill de Isaac Amory et Maria Bapt.
Feb. 6th. Eliz. fille de Adrian Vanhouge et Eliz. Derrick, Bapt.
9th. Feb. Isaac fills de Isaac Lelew et Judeth Leroy, Bapt.

1645 30 Mars Eliz. fill de Isaac Amory et de Ann Morillion Bapt.
Andu Clebaux fill . . . Lenoy Bapt.
John fill de Antoin Le Roux et Maria Duffosse Bapt.
26 Oct. Maur fill de Nicholas Tyssen et Sara Jacob Bapt.
Abraham fill de Anthoine Dubois et de Susann Morrillion Bapt.
Johan fil de Jaques Flahau et Jeanne Castelet Bapt.

1646 Marie fill de Pier Delagaye et Susanne Bapt.
Dina fil de Charles Raney et Sara Elbiet Bapt.
Ann file David Le Conte et de Sara Werquin Bapt.
Isaac fill de Anthoin Massengarbe et Dnia Mitchell Bapt.
Marie file de Marc Dubliq et Eliz. Turquine Bapt.
21 July, Ester fille de Robt Flahau et de Maria Scanflair Bapt.
Eliz. fille de Custar Legrand et de Magdelen Asolom Bapt.
20th Sept. Cath. file Isenbar Scavat et Maria Descamps Bapt.
Marie fil Isaac Roubay et Sarah Scanflair Bapt.
1 Nov. Isaac fill de Isaac Amory et de Ann Morrillion Bapt.
Charles fills Charles Grebault et Eliz. Ferre Bapt.
Abram file Anthoine Merquelier et Bapt.
Sarah file Adrian Vanhouq et de Eliz. Derrick Bapt. (I remember this woman.)

* Same as Beharrel; see Pryme's Diary.

15

1647 Piere fils de Isaac Venin et Cath. Smaque Bapt. 2nd May.
Anne fil Cxtian Fontain et Francoise Beaussart Bapt.
Jacob fils Rolland Dubois et Magdellen Cardoy Bapt.
Margeret fil de Mathin Brugne et de Margueret Bapt.
Isaac Fills Josias Harlay et Maria Legrand Bapt.
Jacob fill Isaac Clais et Maria Deltur Bapt.

1648 Jaques fill Isaac Amory et Ann Morillion Bapt.
Le 4 Oct. Abram fils de Francois Derique et   Bapt.
Le 15 April, David fils de Charles Priam et de Peronne Mesinan, Bapt.
Le May 27, Abram Desquire fils de Abram et de Maria Dubois, Bapt.
Abram Geubau fils de Charles et Eliz. Ferez, Bapt.
Isaac Leleu fils de Jean et de Judith Le Roy, Bapt.
Le Aug 5 Eester Prime fille Guilim et de Sarah Bresme Bapt.
Ester Merquilide fille de Anthoin et Anthennett Treffet, Bapt.
Sarah Smaque fille Chrestien et de Madelener Descay, Bapt.
Oct. 7. Saml. Amory fils de . . . . , Bapt.

1649 Adrien Vanhouq fills de Adrien et de Eliz. Derick, Bapt.
Nov. 18. Susanne Vennin file de Jean et de Cath. Smaque, Bapt.
Jane Benitland file de Thos et Louyse de Zembr, Bapt.

1650 Jaques Dubois fills de Martin et de Judith Salmon, Bapt.
May 5th. David Beharelle fils de Jean et de Jenne Cordain, Bapt.
May 12th. Marie Letalle file de Jean et Judith Descay Bapt.
May 19th. Jenne Leroux file de Anthoine leroux et de Marie Dufosse, Bapt.

1651 11th May. Marie Hancar fille de Isaac et de Jenne Legrand, Bapt.
Ester fille de Robt. et Marie Taffin Bapt.
Susnie (?) Amory fille de Isaac Amory et de Ann Morillion, Bapt.
16 Nov. Ann de Lepiere fille de Joel et Marie Lermitte, Bapt.
Ann Leconte fille de David . . . . Bapt.
25 Jan. David et Abram fils de David and Ester Lenoy, Bapt.

1652 Abram de Lannois fils de Jean et de Marie Pincheon Bapt.
30 May. David Amory fils de Jan et de Marie Thery, Bapt.
Piere de Roubay fils de Jan et de Sara Canster, Bapt.
20 June. Jan filz de Abram Blique et de Marie Discampe, Bapt.
4th Jullet. Piere filz de Daniel Duverlie et de Marye Lenoir, Bapt.
22 Dec. Jacob filz de Jacob Liennar et de Mary Frank, Bapt.
Jacob filz de Charles de Lannoy et de Sara Albert, Bapt.
6 March, Marie file Mr. Berchett Minister de Santoft et Marie Lecoq, Bapt.

1653 Saml. fils de Isaac Amory et de Anne Morillion Bapt.
4 Sept. Isaac filz de Jan Vennin et de Cath. Smaque Bapt.
9 Oct. Vierre filz de Isambar Chauate et Mary Ample, Bapt.

1654 12 Mar. Sarah fille de Joel Lespirre et Mary Lermit, Bapt.
9 April Marye fille de Isaac Lennoy et Marye de Chatlet, Bapt.
25 Jan. Jan fille de Piere Egar et de Sarah Vandebec Bapt.
Jenne fille de Jan demoulin et de Margeret Legraine, Bapt.

1655 Piere filz de Piere Duquenne et de Jenne Bernard Bapt, 19 Aug.

1656 Abram filz de George Hardicq et de Marye Roubay Bapt.
26 May. Piere fils de Sam^{ll}. Letalle et de Eliz. Descon, Bapt.
Abram filz de Simon Le Haire et de Marie Le Roy, Bapt.
Jan filz de Isaac Hancar et de Jenne Legrand, Bapt.

1657 Marie file de Jan Vennin et de Catherin Smaque Bapt.
18 Octr. Marie file Pieire Egar et de Sara Vandebec Bapt.

1658 Sara file de Jan Vennin et Cath. Smaque, Bapt.
Ellie filz de Charles Lennoy et de Sara Albert, Bapt.

1659 Anne file de Jan Lehaire et de Anne Le Roy, Bapt.

1660 25 March Pierre Morillion filz de David Morillion et Ann Letalle, Bapt.
28 Junii, Abram Vennin filz Jan Vennin et Cath Smaque, Bapt.
14 Oct. David Letall filz de Sam^{ll}. Letalle et Eliz. Descon, Bapt.

1661 27 June Susanne file de Benjamin quoy et Elisabet Lehouq, Bapt.

1662 14th Sept. Jan fils de Isaac Beharell et de Marye Bluique, Bapt.

1663 21 Junii. Piere filz de Jan Gougler et de Susanne Herssin, Bapt.

1664 26 Feb. Sara file Abram Brynye et Sara Tissen, Bapt.
1665 5 April, Jaques filz de Jaques Hernu et de Ann Amory, Bapt.
Abram filz de Jaques De Ratt et de Jenne Descamps, Bapt.
1666 Le 20 May, Jaques filz de Jaques Rammery et de Cath. Cigny, Bapt.
4th Julliet, David filz de Jan Egar et Mary Morfin, Bapt.
22nd. Jullet, Jaques filz de Jaques Hernu et Ann Amory, Bapt.
26 Augt Elisabet file de Isaac Deburge et Elizabet Amory, Bapt.
7 Octr. Jacob filz de David Morillion et de Cathrine Benroccdt, Bapt.
11 Novr. Pierre filz Isamber Chavatte et Ann Morrillion, Bapt.
30 Decr. Piere fils de Isaac Vanplue et Jenne de Verlier, Bapt.
1667 19th May. Rebecca file Abram Egard et de Jenne Lennoy, Bapt.
26 May. Isambar filz de Abram Brynye et Sara Tyssens, Bapt.
23 Feb. Pierre filz de Piere Tuyssen et de Elizabet Leenards, Bapt.
1668 Jene file de Jaques Hernu et de Ann Amory.
1669 12 Sept. Piere filz de Piere Leleu et Mary Dumerlye, Bapt.
1670 15 Jan. Piere filz de David Morillion et Cath. Banderete, Bapt.
3 Decr. Isaac filz de Jaques Harnu et de Ann Amory, Bapt.
1671 15 Jan. Abram filz de Matthias Priam et de Sara Smaque, Bapt. It is from this Gent I have collected most of my materials for this Booke.
12 Oct. Penelope filla de Marc Vanvalkenburgh et de Ann Starkey, Bapt.
1672 27 Sept. David filz de David Priam et de Maria Beaumont, Bapt.
6 Mar. Rachel file de Isaac Hanquar et de Jenne Legrand.
9 April. Piere filz de Matthias Priam et de Sara Smacque, Bapt.
1673 24 Feb. Samll. filz de David Letalle et de Marie Amory, Bapt.
6 Mars. Catheline fille de Jan Tyssen et de Susanne Venin, Bapt.
8 May. Jan filz de Jaques Hernu et de Ann Amory, Bapt.
21 June. Jean filz de Francois Oesley et de Marie Amory, Bapt.
8 Jan. David filz de Matthias Priem et de Sara Smaque, Bapt.
8 Feb. Caterine file de Abram Egar et de Jenne de Lannoy, Bapt.
1674 9 April. Susanne file de Abram Brongne et de Sara Tyssen, Bapt.
29 April. Marie fille Gregorii Impson et Susanne Vanpouille, Bapt.
1 Sept. Jan fils de Jan Frouchart et Eliz. Taylor, Bapt.
2 Oct. Jan filz de Jaques Rammery et de Catherine Cugny, Bapt.
Abram filz Jan Swarte et de Jan Dewit, Bapt.
1675 11th Novr. Elis file de Jaques Hernu et de Ann Amory, Bapt.
1 Jan. Anne fille de Isaac Hernu et de Eliz. Amory, Bapt.
1677 8 Jan. Samll. filz de Jaques Hernu et de Ann Amory, Bapt.
1678 4 Decr. Abram filz de Jaques Hernu et de Ann Amory, Bapt.
1681 3d Jan. Isaac filz de Samll. Amory et de Jenne Marequilly, Bapt.
1682 8 Sept. Isaac filz de Jaques Hernu et de Ann Amory, Bapt.
1683 9 Sept. Jan filz de Samll. Amory èt de Jenne Marequilly, Bapt.
1684 20 Novr. Marie fille de Pierre Leleu et Sara Glover, Bapt.
1685 8 June. Susanne fille de Jaques Hernu et de Ann Amory, Bapt.

Burrials.

1650 Marie Dufosse interre a Santoft, 8 Julet.
Piere Derick interre a Santoft, 4 Feb.
1651 Dam Catherin Le Coq de la Femme de Monsr. Berchett Minister, enterr a Santoft, 26 May.

Peter Bontemps, who came from Leyden, was the first pastor. In a letter "done 13th day of June, 1636," he says*: "The participants invited me from Holland and I have dwelt here nearly two years, during which time the number of strangers in this place has increased more than half, and is still daily increasing, the greater part of the new settlers who now appear on the scene come from Normandy and other parts of France."

* Hug. Soc. ii. 296.

M^r. Berchett ministre de Santoft est decede Merquedy 18 Avril 1655 enurion midy et a este enterre le lendemain enuiron 4 heures du soir, a Crowle.
I find Monsr. Berchett's hand at the Churchwardens or Elders accounts to the year 1655, as Pastue of the Church at Santoft.

1659 I find the hand of Jean Dekerhuel Minister a Santoft; and the Monsr. De La prix.
1664 Samuel Lamber, Pasture a Santoft.
1676 Jaques De la Porte, Minister à Sandtoft.
1681 The last minister, Monsr. Le Vaneley. Minister a Santoft.
       Ministers, Monsr. Berchett, Mr. Deckerhuel, Mr. Delaprix, Mr. Delaporte, Mr. Levaneley.

Mem^m. this but an abstract of the Regester. I find above four hundred ninety nine children baptised in this little church, and no doubt many others was baptised in the neighbouring churches of Crowle, Belton, Epworth, Haxey, and Missen, in Lincolnshire, also at Wroot and also at Thorne, Hatfield, Finningley, &c. Their church at Sandtoft being demolished by the Isleanders for severall years, till reedified by Mr. Reading.

N.B.—It was their custome to add the names of the Sureties to every one that was Baptised in the following manner, " Le 25 Feurie 1654, a este Baptises a Red Hall (or a Santoft) Jehan Filz de Pierre Egar et de Sara Vandebec, Ses Tesmoins sont Jehan Egar Filz de Jehan, Marye Quoy femme de Jaques Iserby." (Enquire were Red Hall was.)

665.—The French Colony at Thorney.—Before I proceed to analyze the Baptismal Register, given as an appendix to Mr. Warner's *History of Thorney Abbey* (Leach, Wisbech, 1879), I here reproduce the list of the early immigrants from Santoft. It appears that fourteen whole families moved to Thorney; also some members of twenty-two other families. The notes will shew how long these names were retained at Thorney, and inferentially we may gather who were the most influential people.

The dates following the letter B are when baptisms first and last occur of the names. S signifies that one of the name is entered as a Sponsor. The first entry of any name in this list is the baptism of Marie Flahau, Juin 24, 1655. As might be expected in baptismal registers, some names drop out for a time and then appear again.

Blentiland	Benitland (?)	B. 1664, 1672. [1683.
Blanchart	Blancar	B. 1665, few entries till
Deschamps		B. 1663, 1712.
Egar	Egare, Accar, 1669 (?)	B. 1660, 1717: 22 in all.
Flahau	Flahaut	B. 1657, 1695. Often as S. to 1700.
*Le Haire		B. 1681, 1715.
Hardieg		
†Harley		B. 1655, 1724.
‡De la Haye	De la Haie	B. 1664, 1724.

* Abraham le Haire, Avril 10, 1715.
† There are three separate families of Harley traceable.
‡ Sara de la Haye, Juillet 19, 1724.

De Lespierre	Lepiere, 1685 de le Spiere	B. 1659, 1701 ; S. to 1727.
Massingarbe	Mazingarbe	B. 1656, 1727.
Du Quesne	Desquien, 1670 Descous, 1672	B. 1670. Several S.
Taffin	Tafin	B. 1656. S. in 1675.

Members of 22 other families also came from Santoft. The first names in this list are Susanne Doby, Fev., 1654, and Sara Amory, Aout 19, 1655.

Amory	Amourry, Amaury	B. 1655.
Beharrel	Beharelle	B. 1672, 1696. Many [entries S.
Blique		
Du Bois	Du Bo ; Doby ; Du Boy, 1673	B. 1654 ; many entries to Sep. 1727.
Clairs	Le Cler, 1668 (?) Clair, 1681	Few entries. [S. also.
Le Conte		B. 1660; many till 1711;
Coqueler	Coquelard	S. 1674.
Desbiens	Desbier, 1680, S.	B. 1688, 1711.
Ramery		
Le Roy	(Marie le Roy, wife 1656)	S. 1683, B. 1689, 1720.
Desquiers	Desquin	B. 1666.
*Le Fleur	Flour, generally	B. 1665, 1705 ; S. 1664.
Fontaine		
Frouchart	Frouchard, 1691 Frouchar, 1711–15 Frushar, 1717 Froushar, 1726	B. 1691, 1726. [1703.
Gouy	Gouï, 1695	S. 1656, 1722 ; B. 1661,
Haucer	Hancar, 1657 (?) Hancur, 1660	B. 1657.
Le Lieu	Le Loue, 1659	
Marquillier	Morquilly, Mequily, Merquillier, 1690	B. 1666 ; few till 1717 ; S. 1727.
Renard	Renan, S. 1670 Renaud, 1694 Le Renan, 1667	B. 1694, 1699 ; S. 1707.
Le Roue	De la Rue, 1660 (Roux ?) Rou, 1706	Many to 1725.
Le Talle	Le Tal (Anne le Talle, wife 1656)	B. 1657, 1714 ; S. to 1725.
De Lanoy	De la Noy, Lannoy	B. 1661, 1705. About 20 entries ; several S. to 1724.
Vennin (wife, 1662)	Venins, 1690, S. . . . (? Vermin, 1669)* (? Hennin, 1665)	B. 1695, 1711 ; S. 1725.

Throughout this register the maiden name of the wife is given, and the father's surname follows the child's christian name ; also in every case the names of the male and female sponsors, thus :—

* For marriage of Anthoine Leflour at Santoft, 1645, see Art. 652, p. 324.

* Vermin, found several times in the printed Register, must be a misprint. Vienin, 1643, in Santoft Register; also Vennin, 1644. Many other refugees joined this French community very soon after their settlement here, such as Le Fevre (B. 1655), Le Pla (B. 1655), Ugille (B. 1656) afterwards (?) Usill (Usille, B. 1674), names still retained in the district; also de Bailleu (B. 1659) now Bayley, Milleville (B. 1660), Merkillier (B. 1689), Holmes (B. 1657), Grome (B. 1656).

† I was much puzzled with the heading of this column in Mr. Warner's book. He has "child's Christian name" only, whereas it is the child's Christian name and father's surname. I do not find any double Christian name in the register.

‡ This name is in Thorney list as early as 1660; no father's name.

DATE.	† CHILD'S NAME.	PARENTS.	SPONSORS.
1655 Juin 24	Marie Flahau	Jacques et Jenne du Shattelot	Marc le Pla Marie Massingarbe
1657 Aoust. 8	Susanne Blancart	Antoine et Jenne de le Spiere	Lievin Morrier Susanne Gouy

There is an exception in 1682: Jacques Halo; Jean et sa femme.

In many cases the child has the Christian name of the sponsor. The Santoft register (Art. 652) does not shew the same uniformity, but the wife's maiden name is there always given, as :—

1652. Abram de Lannois fils de Jean et de Marie Pincheon,‡ Bapt.

1657. Marie file Pieire Egar et de Sara Vandebec, Bapt.

I find one instance, in 1671, in which the surname of the mother only could be given, and then the child took the christian name of the female sponsor.

Twins were registered, *i.e.*, Piere and Ester Egar, in 1668; Jeanne and Ester Sigé, in 1688; Esther and Pierre Lisy, in 1690; Marie and Daniel Clays (mother Ester de Lespierre) in 1695; Marguerite and Sara Le Pla, in 1696; Jonathan and David Bailleut, in 1696; Isaac and Jacob Garbaut, in 1699; Joseph and Benjamin le Roy, in 1703; Elizabeth and Mary de la Haye, in 1707; Elizabeth and Susanne Goglar, in 1707; Marie and Susanne du Pont, in 1708; 11 cases in all.

Triplet: 1713, Marie, Elie, and Susanne Bakley; parents, Elie (Bakley) et Jeanne Wilson; each child had two separate sponsors.

The sponsorship among these people seems to have been religiously observed, in fact, it was a veritable system of guardianship.

I have made a separate entry of all dates of individual sponsors, but too detailed to be reproduced here. The following names appear most frequently as sponsors: Beharrel, Le Conte, Flahau, Gouy, Harley, De la Haye, De Lanoy, De Lespierre, Massingarbe, Marquillier, Du Quesne, Taffin, Le Talle; next to these Du Bois (Du Bo, Doby, &c.) and Flour.

The following table gives the number of baptisms in each year.

DATE.	M.	F.	DATE.	M.	F.	DATE.	M.	F.
1654	1	3	1684	16	11	1714	4	8
1655	5	11	1685	8	19	1715	5	6
1656	16	10	*1686	7	20	1716	3	1
1657	18	23	1687	18	11	1717	8	5
1658	4	3	1688	12	13	1718	5	3
1659	22	20	1689	13	9	1719	1	5
1660	14	25	1690	7	10	1720	2	6
1661	17	18	1691	10	17	1721	5	0
1662	10	21	1692	12	12	1722	4	2
1663	23	26	1693	7	10	1723	3	3
	130	160		110	132		40	39
1664	17	18	1694	10	4	1724	6	3
1665	24	22	1695	18	11	1725	2	4
1666	16	21	1696	11	14	1726	3	2
1667	21	18	1697	12	11	1727	4	4
1668	21	16	1698	10	8			
1669	17	21	1699	12	15		15	13
1670	10	13	1700	13	11			
1671	18	17	1701	19	6	TOTALS.		
1672	22	17	1702	11	7			
1673	22	19	1703	9	13	DATE.	M.	F.
	197	182		125	100	1654 to 63	130	160
1674	18	18	1704	9	16	to 73	197	182
1675	15	21	1705	17	9	to 83	134	126
1676	16	9	1706	8	8	to 93	110	132
1677	16	7	1707	10	16	1703	125	100
1678	12	11	1708	10	10	to 13	93	108
1679	9	18	1709	12	13	to 23	40	39
1680	6	7	1710	8	11	to 27	15	13
1681	9	17	1711	5	11			
1682	22	9	1712	9	6		844	860
1683	11	9	1713	5	8	= 1704 Baptisms.		
	134	126		93	108	25 entries were lost.		

* In 1686, 14 girls in succession.

From this register, the colony would appear to have been most flourishing in the second decade, i.e., from 1664 to 1673, and to have declined at the beginning of the eighteenth century. Then it seems to have migrated or became gradually blended with the neighbouring population. Mr. Warner remarks :—"The merging of the settlers with their English fellow parishioners eventually rendered a separate ecclesiastical establishment unnecessary, and the Baptismal Register ceases to be distinct from the English register, Oct. 3, 1727."

It would be interesting to obtain as full a list as possible of those, now in the district, who can claim descent from these interesting people. Wells speaks of the De la Pryme family. Matthew emigrated from Ypres, in Flanders, during the persecution of the Duke d'Alva (? 1666), and settled at Hatfield Chase soon after it was drained by Vermuyden. Prime, Priam, and Priem, occur in the Santoft register. Matthew de la Pryme had a son born at Hull, the Rev. Abraham Pryme, who became Minister of Thorne. Of him Mr. Wells remarks, " How interesting and affecting a narrative would Abraham De la Pryme, the antiquary and philosopher of the Levels, have produced had he lived to perfect his admirable design of giving a complete history of this singular colony! We read with peculiar pleasure the simple and touching inscription on the monument of Matthew De la Pryme, in the Church at Hatfield." He died at the age of 34 years; but I have not found the words inscribed on the monument. Can Mr. Egar supply this inscription?

Lowestoft. S. H. MILLER.

678.—Vermuyden and the Walloon Colonies.—Having been engaged for some time past in an examination and analysis of the Baptismal Register of the French Colony, settled at Thorney, (the entries began 1 Feb., 1654, and ended 3 Oct., 1727,) I have been led to the conclusion that Cornelius Vermuyden was instrumental in bringing those French-speaking people to the Fens. Notwithstanding what has appeared in Art. 564, touching the work of this great engineer, I cannot make my position clear without entering into further details.

Vermuyden's first visit to this country seems to have been prior to his undertaking the work of repairing the Thames banks at Dagenham, in 1621. In his *Discourse*, written in 1642,* he does not give the date of his first visit, but remarks:—

> When K. James, of blessed memory, undertooke the drayning, as aforesaid (*i.e.* of the Great Fennes), at that time I was come over into England invited to this work. I took several views thereof, went away, returned, and reviewed the same, took advice of the experienced men of the Low Countries, and from time to time did study how to contrive that work for the best advantage, being at that time in proposition to have undertaken the doing of that said work, together with my friends at our own charge, for a proportion of the land.

Wells (Vol. I., pp. 92-3) says:—

> But the first exertions of this very extraordinary man, did not take place within the Great Level of the Fens. It is said, that prince Henry, eldest son of James I., making a progress to York, hunted at Hatfield Chase, near Doncaster, and was entertained by one Portington of Tudworth. Vermuyden was in the Suite of this prince; and hence, it is conceived, arose the design of draining those Levels. Having obtained a grant from the crown of all its property, Vermuyden entered into the prosecution of that great undertaking with all the confidence which a knowledge of what had been executed in Holland, and a natural genius

* See this *in extenso* in Appendix XVII. of Wells's *History and Drainage of the Great Level of the Fens*, 1830.

for vast designs, could inspire. His own command of capital was scarcely adequate to the object in contemplation; but he was supported by many of his countrymen, particularly by Sir Philibert Vernatti, the Volkenburgh family, the Vampereens, Abram Vernatti, Andrew Bocean and John Corsellis. Some of these embarked with Vermuyden in this design, and subsequently in the scheme for draining the Great Level.

But prince Henry died 6 Nov., 1612 ; and this was nine years before Vermuyden was employed on the Thames banks. The scheme for draining Hatfield Chase was, no doubt, sanctioned by James I., but not fully entered on till after that king's death ; *i.e.* not till 1626. In 1629, Vermuyden was knighted, and then took a grant from the crown for the whole of Hatfield Chase.

The persecutions at that time felt by the people of the Low Countries, on the Continent, induced many to seek an asylum elsewhere. In the United Provinces, only Calvinists could hold offices of state. In Flanders the Roman Catholic religion was dominant, and the provisions of the Edict of Nantes were violated under various pretexts long before Cardinal Richelieu succeeded, in 1629, in bringing the French protestants to a state of subjection. All the industrious and thrifty people, who could, availed themselves of every opportunity of finding employment in free England. They do not appear to have suffered any disability through the changes of government in England. Mr. Warner quotes Gregorio Leti *(Teatro Britannico)* to this effect:—

> Charles II., reigning king, with his habitual incomparable kindness, granted privileges to the French population; among others, a church, which had 500 communicants. Every Sunday there were services in English and French. For the latter language there was a Minister named Michael David, of Geneva, a person of learning and great zeal.

Hence the settlement of the French-speaking people (their exact nationality cannot be defined) at Santoft in Hatfield Chase, may be attributed to Vermuyden and those associated with him as leaders.†

But the time came when opposition from the natives of Yorkshire led to another migration, in part at least. We come to the time of the Commonwealth. Five years after the death of King Charles I., part of the colony withdrew from Hatfield Chase. Vermuyden was then employed in the Fens. "In 1654, he joined in the conveyance of land in Hatfield Level." This was his last transaction in that district. In that *same year* we find the French Colony at Thorney, and although I know of no specific record, I infer they came there through the advice and influence of Vermuyden.

Lowestoft. S. H. MILLER.

706.—Strangers in Hatfield Level, 1636.—The work of Vermuyden at Hatfield Chase, and the relationship between the French-speaking settlers there and those in the neighbourhood of Thorney, and the great similarity between the difficulties, obstructions, and ultimate success, of the drainage operations at the lowlands in Yorkshire and those at the Fenland district with which our readers are best acquainted, will justify our devoting a few pages to a notice of some of the early experiences of the strangers at Hatfield Level.

Archbishop Neile's account of the immigrants employed about the drainage of Hatfield Level shews how hard was the pioneer life of the Protestant alien. He lived in a hovel and browsed on coleseed. The Primate looked with no favour on the Stranger Church. In 1634 His Grace assailed the community at Canterbury. "They are like tipplers in a tavern. They come in and eat of the fat of the land, and shall they not conform?" In vain did the ministers testify their desire to live in union with the Church of England. Conformity was the darling of Archbishop Laud's heart. This harsh treatment of the strangers occasioned an article in his impeachment. The Archbishop of York did his utmost to further the policy of the Primate. He offered the Common Prayer in French to M. Bontemps, one of the Ministers: but there seems to have been no printed translation before the version of Mr. Durell, Minister of the Savoy after the Restoration. A little patience and all would have ended well. In the next year a Minister willing to use the Common Prayer appeared. This may have been Mr. Berchett, who was born at Crowle.

This letter is from the State Papers, Dom. Series, Car. I. 327, 47:—

Salutem in Christo.

May it please yor Grace to pardon me if I trouble you with a longer letter then perhaps you would expect. And to begin with those thanks which I owe you, for your great love and favour which you shewed to our Church of York at ye hearing of the cause betwixt ye Church and ye Cittie; and I humbly pray your Grace to doe me this favour to present my most humble and bounden service to his sacred Matie and dutifull acknowledgement of his exceeding great goodness manifested to our Church at his Royall hearing and Gracious ordering of that cause.

I make bould to acquaint your Grace with a business of importance, as I thinke, much concerning both the State and the Church, which I knew not of till this my coming into the country, which is this—I finde that y^e drayners of the Levell of Hatfield Chace doe not imploy any

Above: The Fens in full flood.
Below: Pleasant river scene.

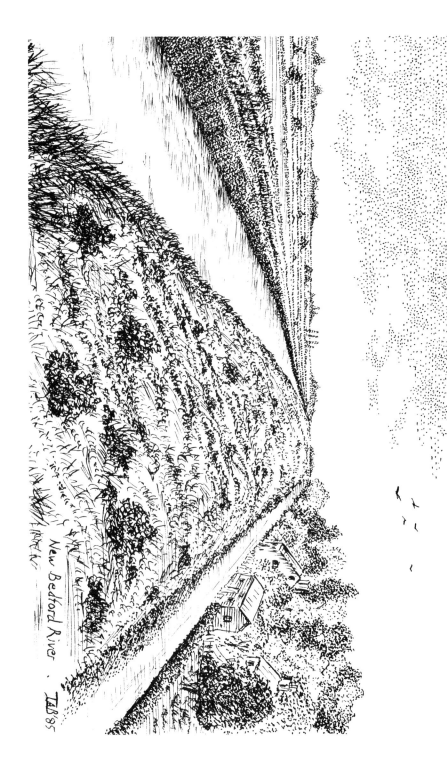

Englishmen, that I can heare of, in the husbanding of those grounds, but altogether imploy Frenchmen and a few Dutchmen who come into the kingdome daily in great numbers, and are already become a plantation of some two hundred families, and more are daily expected to come by shipsfulls. I heare there is at present a shipfull at Hull yet unloaded, and another ship-ful is said to be at Harwich of the same kinde. This new plantation hath been on foote for some yeares past, and they have sett up among themselves the Forme and discipline of ye French Church. A barne of Sir Phillibert Vernatty is ye place which they use for their Church, whither the whole company have resort on Sondaies: where they baptize in a dishe after their owne manner, and administer the Sacrament after their homely fashion of sitting. For their Government they have their Consistorye of the Minister, three being Elders, and three Deacons. The place or barne wherein they performe their divine service is on the very edge of Lincolnshire adjoyning upon Yorkshire; by advantage whereof they pretend license given them by ye Bishop of Lincoln *non in scriptis sed verbotenus*, to have their exercises of Religion according to the forme of the French Church as it is permitted to French and Dutch in other parts of the Realme.

Their Minister, who hath been with them these two yeares, is one Peter Bontemps, admitted into the ministry, as he saieth, by ye French ministers at Leyden. I have spoken with him, and from his mouth I have the effect of that I have before written. I make bould to send yor Grace a letter of his which he wrote to ye Sharers of ye Levell, whereby yor Grace will see how it is indevored to bring ye forme of ye French Church into England, which I shall ever to ye uttermost of my power oppose; and I trust his Sacred Matie will uphold me herein and inhable me to bring them to ye practise of our booke of Common Prayer & none other, they being permitted to have ye use thereof in ye French tongue; whereof they may have as many books already printed as they can desire.

I think yor Grace can remember how that one day I made knowne to the Lords of the Counsell y^t Sir Phillibert Vernatty had mooved me for my favour that ye strangers y^t dwelt upon his levell might build a Chappell for ye exercise of divine service: whereto I answered I would assoure them all lawfull favour so as they would conforme themselves to ye Church of England: otherwise not. At which time I alsoe mooved their Lordships for their favour that if Sir Phillibert should at any time moove their Lordships to any other purpose, their Lordships would second me in my resolution and answer given to him in this business: of which my motion their Lordships well allowed. And I beseech yor Grace to moove his Matie to uphold me herein that neither Sir Phillibert nor any other may obtaine anything of his Matie to ye contrary.

It seemeth that upon ye answere y^t I gave to Sir Phillibert he finding how nere Lincoln diocese bordered upon Yorkshire made his recourse to my Lord of Lincoln, hoping to finde that favour of him which I had denied, and perhaps obtained as much as is aforesaid. I heard they have burned bricks and are preparing materials to build a Chapple there in Lincoln diocese to which all ye inhabitants of ye levell though dwelling in my diocese might repaire: bout I shall, by ye grace of God, prohibit those that live in my diocese to go thither. I am verie confident that yor Grace doth favour me in this my resolution and will assist me in constrayning to conforme themselves to ye Church of England.

I leave to his Matys consideracon with what conveniency and safety to this State such a plantation should be permitted to be of strangers, men of very mean condition, that upon advantage may become as vipers nourished in our bosomes, that take the bread out of the mouths of English subjects by overbidding them in rents of land and doing more work for a groat than an Englishman can do for sixpence. If your Grace did know in what cottages these people live and how they fare for foode you would wonder at it.

I shall be glad to receive such answer as you shall thinke good to returne me.   Your Graces very loving frend & brother
    from Southwell. 23 Junii 1636.   B. Ebor^{r}.

The Bishop of Lincoln probably altered his mind : for the strangers were selling, in 1637, the materials they had provided for the new chapel, and many were looking about for pastures new. This seems to have been the occasion of the petition for their settlement in Gualtres Forest: but something more was necessary to establish a community and endow a church than "good intentions" on the part of the petitioners : there seems to be nothing further known about this forest "plantation."

To the Kings most excellent Matie

The humble peticon of Robert Long and John Gibbon shewing that after the draining of the Levell of Hatfeild Chace in the countie of York, most of the participants, being Dutch, brought over divers French families out of Normandy and other parts of France being all protestants, and planted them as undertenants in the greatest part of the said levell, where they have since continued, and are very honest and industrious people and very good tenants.

The petn^{rs} shew further that they are by purchase become yor Ma^{tys} feefarmers of the lands of the late disaforrested forrest of Gualtres in the said county of York, and that the same being wild barren and unmanured they can make no considerable benefit thereof but by leasing it to undertenants that will bestow charges and use industry to reduce those lands to tillage, and that the people of the countrey adjacent either out of combination or wilfulness will not take the same to pay any considerable rent for that they say the same have been their Commons, though your Ma^{ty} hath allowed them great proportions in lieu of their commons.

Wherefore yor petn^{rs} are constrained to bring some of the french tenants out of the said levell of Hatfeild Chace who being industrious men and skilful in the manuring of grounds doe offer such rates to the petn^{rs} for the land as are reasonable, and because the lands of the said forrest ly remote from all townes the petn^{rs} intend at their owne charge to erect convenient houses for the tenants, and to build a church for them, if they may obtaine such authority from yor Ma^{ty} as shall be necessary in this behalfe: and because none of the said french doe yet understand English perfectly the petn^{rs} have found out a minister who is beneficed in this countrey who speaketh good french and is willing to do all divine offices in that language to the said tenants and shall therein conforme himselfe to the laudable discipline ceremonies and government of the Church of England, and use no other forme of praier there but the Common prayer of the Ch. of England but in the french tongue, and the petn^{rs} will endow the said Church with the annual revenue of 100^{li} for ever.

The petn^{rs} therefore humbly beseech yor Ma^{ty} to grant unto them licence to found a Church there which may be presentative for ever in which divine service & sermons may be exercized in the french tongue, and to settle lands & tythes in mortmain to the parson and his successors there to be presented, and to signifie yor royall pleasure to the Lo. Archbp. of Yorke his Grace that such a minister may be admitted for the present to use the french tongue in the exercise of his said function according to the institution of the Church of England, until those french which shall inhabit there shall by their conversacon attayne to the perfect understanding of the English.

And your petn^{rs} shall ever pray &c.

This last is without date. It was probably presented on the same day that the following order was made.

   At the Court at Whitehall. 6 June 1637.

  His Maty approving the good intentions of the petnrs in the building of the Church in the place proposed is pleased that Mr. Atturney General prepare such licinces for the erecting thereof and settling a provision of maintenance in mortmaine of 100li per ann. to the parson & his successors to be there presented by his Maty and his successors for ever as may be fit for his royal signature. And his Maty holding it fit to allow the inhabitants the celebration of Divine Service in a language they understand, is likewise pleased to grant licence that it shalbe read in the french tongue, but in the forme of the liturgy of the Church of England, and likewise that they may have sermons in the french language according to the Articles & Canons of the Church of England till the inhabitants shall attaine to the understanding of English, and then the said service & sermons to be in the English tongue according to the forme articles & canons aforesaid. And the Lo. Archbp. of Yorke his grace is to give allowance and institution to such a minister, he finding him conformable to the religion & discipline here established.

  The mass of the strangers were dwelling in the Level in 1655 when Pasteur Jean de Kerhuel with some fifty of the community petitioned the Protector to save them from the violence of rioters who a second time had assembled with guns and other weapons, and had beaten down the windows, doors, seats, and pulpit of their church, laid them in a heap, and set them on fire.   L. GACHES.

  765.—Aliens in the Fens.—The influx of the French at the Revocation of the Edict of Nantes in 1685 did not add materially to the number of foreigners in the Fens. The Huguenots, chiefly artizans, settled where work was to be found. There were thousands in London. There was a colony at Canterbury, where they found a congregation of Walloons that had been established in the reign of Edward VI. The Royal Lutestring Company employed 5000 in weaving silks at Spitalfields. There was a branch of the Company at Ipswich, and to this source many of the French names found in Suffolk may be traced: and Dutch and Walloon congregations had been established at Norwich since 1568.* In 1681 R. Bonhomme, a French merchant, was induced to transfer his linen drapery business to England. In that year the Secretary of State was informed, by H. Saville from Paris, that "M. Bonhomme will be able to give you some lights as to the bringing the manufacture of sail cloth into England, a project the Government are so fond of." At that time the English fleet was dependent on the weavers of

Brittany and Normandy for canvas.† Bonhomme brought his looms and his weavers to Ipswich, and made sail-cloth for the fleet. The bulk of the silk weavers came to Ipswich somewhat later. On 28th Nov., 1693, the Corporation resolved :— "That 50 families of French Protestants who make lutestring shall be admitted to this town and they shall have 20^s each family and their charges of coming to the town shall be found by the Town and they shall have a church minded for them and 20£ a year for their minister for 2 years and they shall not be rated or put into any office for seven years ; and that Mr. Snelling shall go to London to treat with the Frenchmen about this business." The Royal Lutestring Company was chartered ; so the reports of their Secretary, Mr. H. Reneu, are found among the Treasury Papers, with the names of the workmen employed at Ipswich.

Names are not a safe index of the origin of a family. There were families in France of Scotch origin, whose ancestors had been in the Scotch body guard of the King of France, and these came to England. A valuable work, relating to these families, is *Les Ecossais en France* by Francisque Michel, published by Trubner & Co. in 1862. During the Commonwealth the Council of State, in 1653, resolved that "the Prisoners Committee do consider how the Dutch prisoners taken in the last fight may be disposed of. That the Committee do agree with the Company of Adventurers in the Fens for taking off as many Dutch prisoners as they require to use in their work paying them as ordinary labourers."

And by the Act of 1654, for the preservation of the works of the Great Level of the Fens, all purchasers, being foreign

---

* The Walloons, a French speaking people of the Netherlands, were settled first at Sandwich, removed thence to Norwich in 1568. They restored the manufacture of wool fabrics, which was lost to Norwich by the ravages of the Black Death in 1348-9.

The Register, of the Walloon Church, which dates from 1595, is entitled :—

C^e lijure commence le 22 de Juyn l'an de grase 1595 et pour le batem des enfans de leglijge Walloughe de la vijlle de Nordvijt regijdigyant en icelle vijlle et alors en ce tems la mestre Thomas Laijert en maijeur de la vijlle.

The Walloon congregation was dissolved in 1832. The Church estate, by a decree in Chancery made in 1839, is devoted :—

1. To keeping the church of Little St. Mary's, Norwich, and the monuments and tombs in repair.
2. To apply £50 per ann. in apprenticing out poor boys of Norwich, giving a preference to children of French Protestant origin.
3. The balance to be paid to the French Protestant Hospital in London, conditionally that at least two inmates should always be received and kept there on the nomination of the trustees of the Norwich French Church Charity, who should give preference in such nomination to descendants of French Protestants who or whose families were or had been resident in Norwich.

† In 1699 our imports from France exceeded £1,000,000; of this, buckram, dowlas, and canvas amounted to £462,000.

protestants, of fen lands were to be accounted free denizens of the Commonwealth. Who can doubt that many of these foreigners decided for England just as some of the French prisoners at Norman Cross did early in this century? To the latter source families at Stilton named Habart and Teslof may be traced, and Nurse,* a French subaltern, married an attorney's daughter and settled there.

The origin of many Walloon families in the Fens may be traced to Thorney. Jamblin originates from M. Jembelin, a minister of the Walloon community at Thorney. There was another minister, Jean de M. Jemblin, of St. Pierre sur Dives, who on 27th March, 1685, received from "S.M. Louis XIV permission de se retirer en Angleterre." He was the author of an essay "on the validity of Geneva Orders," and pastor at St. Clement, Jersey, where he died in 1712. The Anglican Church insisted on Episcopal Ordination. Dean Whittingham of Durham, a fugitive reformer in Queen Mary's reign, who held Geneva Orders, was in "a parlous state." His death saved him from deprivation. Then foreign protestants looked askance at Roman Orders. In 1646 the Colloque refused to recognize the Congregation at Whittlesey, and their pastor, Du Perrier, on the ground that it was not sanctioned by the Crown as was that of Thorney.* The minute of the Colloque is this :—

> Le sieur du Perrier soi disant pasteur, ayant présenté lettres de la part des frères de Whittlesey aux fins d'être incorporés en nos Eglises, la Campagnie ne voulant entrer pour le present en l'examen de la personne et ordination du dit sieur, a répondu qu'elle ne pouvait accorder cette demande jusqu'a ce que l'autorité suprême lui donne fondement.

Du Perrier was in Roman Orders. However, in 1656, the Cœtus without insisting on re-ordination received him into the Association "pour donner plus d'autorité a ses labeurs et calmer les scrupules des fideles de Southampton," where he officiated as pastor after the Whittlesey congregation was united to Thorney. The Church of England did her best to aid the distressed French ministers, but the English tongue is not acquired all at once: so they had to be stowed away in out of the way parishes. Mr. Pujolas† found his way to Parson Drove. His stipend must have been slender. In 1696 the Commissioners for Pious Uses held an inquiry at Wisbech

---

* There is also a Huguenot family of this name.

touching the rents and profits of lands given and appointed for the maintenance of the Chaplain. The jurors found "that several writings relating to the Chapel of Parson Drove are withheld by the late chapel-wardens; that the profits of a messuage and divers parcels of land in Leverington and Parson Drove, containing 141 acres, and 11 acres of marsh land have been held and enjoyed and disposed of by the chapel-wardens of the said hamlet; and that there has been misimployment in 1690 by Robert Ball chapel warden who received rents £64 . 10^s. 2^d, and accounted only for 20£ paid to the minister; and a like misimployment in 1692, by Jeremiah England and Thos. Sweetland; and in 1693 by John Roper and John Pales."

Probably Mr. Pujolas' income was augmented by a sum from the Royal Bounty. In 1717 there is an entry of a grant to H. Pujolas Junr 53, wife and 9 children . £18.*

L. G.

809.—Drainage of Thorney Fen.

Long before the settlement of the Walloons at Thorney, the skill of the inhabitants of Flanders about drainage works had attracted the attention of the Commissioners of Sewers, who were supervising the drainage of "surrounded grounds" in the fenland. In 1588, an Act of the Privy Council* recites that the Commissioners "had in chardgable sorte endevored divers workes of sewers whereuppon small effectes had proceeded." And the Council appointed as aids to the Commissioners, "Humfrey Bradley of Bergen-ap-Zome, John Hexhame of Huntingdon gent. and Ralfe Agasse † of Suffolk men able to make viewe and platt for the several fennes marshes and decaied grounds in the said fower shires and to observe the true dyssentes of waters and qualyties of the soile through which waters should be carryed."

* By the rule of the Walloon Churches in England, the Bishop of the Diocese, as Superintendent, was informed of the choice of a minister by the congregation, and his approval was necessary before formal appointment. For the appointment of minister of the French Church at Soho, London, the licence of the Crown is necessary. This is the only foreign Protestant Church in London which has retained the Presbyterian discipline.

† T.P. xxxv. 7. Liste des Ministres Francois necessiteux refugiés en Angleterre 1695. Thos. Henry Pujolas, 32 ans. The Register dates from 1599. Some of the inhabitants bore Flemish names, e.g., Leehoy, Couard, Delahay. Moses Pujolas, naturalized in 1696, was the first secretary of the General Assembly of the French Churches which were established in London in 1720 "pour la paix et pour l'ordre dans notre refuge." D. C. Agnew, in *Protestant Exiles from France* (3rd Ed. 1886), says that Mr. P. was minister of the French Church of Parson Drove, and gives the year of his death 1749. On 5 Dec., 1691, in Le Quarré French Church, Little Dean Street, London, Henry Pujolas, ck., was married to Anne Richer. In 1704, Ensign Denys Pujolas of the Foot Guards was wounded at the battle of Schellenberg. In 1734 he was Lieut. Colonel in Sir Charles Hotham's regiment. Henry Pujolas, Esq., the son of John Pujolas, held the office of Richmond Herald. He died in 1764, aged 31.

It was as early as 1574 that Sir William Russell‡ sought to arrange with certain Protestants in Flanders to cross the channel and reclaim the surrounded grounds at Thorney. His petition to the Privy Council of Queen Elizabeth is as follows:—

The humble request of Sir William Russell Knight to the right honorable the Lords of her Maty'ˢ Prevy Councell.

Humbly besecheth yor honorable Lordshipps That whereas yor Lo's. suppliant is seased of an estate of inheritance of a great quantitie of mearrishe & drowned grounds late parcells of the possessions of the

* Acts of P. C., 21 March, 1588.
† In the Register of the Norwich Walloon Church this name is spelt Agache.
‡ A Commissioner of Sewers in 1574. Sir William was 4th son of Francis, 2nd Earl of Bedford. He was created Baron Russell, of Thornhaugh, in 1603, and died in 1613. His only son Francis succeeded to the Earldom in 1627.

Monastery of Thorney in the Countie of Cambridge* wch at this present are more charge then profitt to yoʳ suppliant and greatlie in daunger with their waters in extremities, the partes of Holland in the countie of Lincolne and the Soacke of Wisbiche in the Isle of Elye. Soe it is right honorable that certaine persons of good abillitie & skille in draynynge of mearrishe grounds dwellinge within Northe Hollande beyoande the seas havinge vewed the same grounds woolde inhabite those wastes and remove themselves frome their owne cuntrie and endevor the recoverie thereof in some measure upon certeine condicons to be agreed upon between yor suppliant and them, wherewith all they doe require that those previleges followinge mighte also bee obtained in their behalfe from her Matie by yor honorable meanes.

Imprimis that all the encrease that shall be gotten within the said lande by their great industrye and travill maie bee frome thence carried or transported to any parte or ports within this realme or to marketts ffaires or martts, maie bee free frome the Queene's takers and of prises sett by her Matʸˢ Officers either within liberties or without.

Item that the inhabitants nor their servaunts their abidinge bee not prest to serve in the warrs beyond the seas for fortie yeres ensuinge but onlie within the lande.

Item that in regarde of their great chardges in gayninge those drowned grounds and in buildinge uppon the same there maye be an assent frome yoʳ LLs. and by yoʳ hon. meanes frome her Matʸ that they maie be excepted in anie parliaments for tenne yeres ensuinge forthe of acts for subsidewes and that the rate of the tennths and fifteenths now assessed upon the Toune or lymites of Thorney maie bee contynewed onlie withoute raisinge the same to anie higher rate.

If my good LL. these Hollanders maie bee brought to inhabite that place wch nowe is desolate & unprofitable they will by their successe industrie and skill greatlie encorage the inhabitants adjoyninge who are now doubtful or careless, by their examples to take the like endevors within their continent of mearrishe groundes wch are deemed by men of arte in measuringe to be above five hundred thousand acres wherebie there would ensewe a great encrease of people & wealth within those parts now accompted the weakest place for able personnes or wealthie men within this realme.

The petition was referred to the crown lawyers,† who gave their opinion that "All these be matters concerning the State then matters of law for us to deal in, saving for the leases to be made to these strangers which may not be good unless they become denizens."

* The grant of the site of the Monastery to John Lord Russell was in 1549. It included about 7,000 acres of ground in Karr fenn, Mary's fenn, Torrers and le Gores fenns, and farms at Thorney Barre and Northey.
† J. Popham, Attorney General; J. Egerton, Solicitor General.

Objection was raised that the privileges sought for could not be granted by letters patent, and that an Act of Parliament would be necessary. Nothing was done. It was not till 1630 that the Earl of Bedford engaged in the scheme for the drainage of the Great Level of the Fens; and at that time it seems that the Hollanders were lured to cast in their lot with Vermuyden and the "Participants," who had undertaken the drainage of Hatfield Chace; but there were a good many Walloons about Whittlesey and Thorney in 1650, when Sandtoft church was destroyed, and the strangers migrated to Thorney.* Sir Theodore Turquet de Mayerne, a French Protestant, physician to King James I. in 1611, obtained a grant of several thousand acres of fen ground at Whittlesey, and many of the Walloon families of that district owe their change of domicile to the drainage scheme of Sir Theodore. The Minister of the strangers was maintained by an acreage charge of 12$d.$ on the ground cultivated by members of the community, provided that he was not to receive more than £80 a year. He found it difficult to collect £50. The agents of the Earl of Bedford induced many of these strangers to hold land at Thorney, and they then contributed to the church there. Perhaps there was no rent to pay. The soil was poor enough. In 1622, one of the Commissioners of Sewers, who resided near Peterborough, describes Thorney fen as "a black spongy meere holding water and only dried by summer's heat. It breeds no good grass and the soil so cold and spongy that a beast lying thereon will rise again wet sided and yet no water to be seen." He thought drainage would never pay, "for nothing can drive tenants thither but extremity of drought." He did not reckon with the Walloon. Many had sunk good money in that fen.† "An experiment was made to burn fodder for ashes to make allome and to that end certain persons bought the crop of 3000 acres of the best fodder ground at 12$s.$ an acre yet they are vanished with the smoke and do hazard no more." The only good word the Commissioner has is for Barr Pasture. That was good ground.‡

* G. Du Perier, a Protestant Minister, was at Whittlesey in 1646. Peter Bontemps, minister at Sandtoft, came with his flock to Thorney. In 1682, Michael David, of Geneva, was at Thorney.

† S.P. Dom. Jac. I. 128. This Commissioner was the author of some verses which have been attributed to Mr. Fortrey.

‡ Barr Pasture farm adjoins Willow Hall farm. These farms were occupied by Walloon families for a long time. The Builleuls or Baillys of Willow Hall have been chronicled by Judge Bailly, of Westminster County Court, who presided on the Bench when 90 years of age. It might be expected that the strangers would have introduced some Dutch or French terms in the vernacular of the Fens. Thirty years ago the retort of "a breedling" was, "I count it's all your flummery," *i.e.*, tricks, for which the French is "flannerie": but "flummery" was in use in the 16th century.

A less gloomy view of Thorney and the work of the settlers there is given by Gregorio Leti in his history of Great Britain, entitled "Teatro Brittanico." It appears that the Earl of Bedford sought to obtain the approval of King Charles II. to the settlement of strangers at Thorney by presenting his Majesty with a team of red deer, the principal inhabitants of the Isle. Leti* thus refers to the circumstance :—

Quando il Signor Conte di Bedford prese la risolutione di dar queste terre per farle dissecare; trovo una curiosa inventione, havendo fatto domare sei de' piu grossi cervi, col tenerli chiusi per qualche tempo, in un continuo strepito di tamburri, usolini e altri instromenti, che domati con questo mezo, e apparecchiati al tiro d'una carozza, ne fece poi presente al Re' Carlo primo.

"When the Earl of Bedford determined to drain the land he adopted the strange device of training six of the largest deer and keeping them shut up some time he tamed them by the constant sounding of drums harps and other instruments then harnessed them like a set of coach horses and presented them to the King Charles I."

A coach and six stags would attract a good deal of attention jingling down Whitehall, harnessed tandem fashion. The royal licence was enough to warrant the settlement of the Walloons. The King could exempt them from the Ecclesiastical control by virtue of his Royal Supremacy; little else was wanted; the Muster master was unlikely to look for recruits at Thorney.† They "planted" themselves there and the Earl took care of them.

Leti describes their practice of burning the peat in order to make it productive, and he notices the introduction of coleseed.

Dissecarono una bona parte di terra, la coltivarono et vi comincarono a seminare certi Cavoli Selvatici detti Colzat da quali se ne cava certo oglio che serve molto non solo per la lampa ma per quei che lavorono in lana.

"They have drained a good quantity of land, and have cultivated it, and therein have sown a kind of wild colewort

---

* An able Italian who writes in an easy style. The homes and habits of the English people are well described in his "Teatro"; but it gave offence to the Court, and was vigorously suppressed. It is in 2 volumes. 4°: London, 1682: dedicated to "Carlo II monarca invincibile nell' oceano Re di Inghilterra." There is a Flemish edition, 5 vols. 8°, 1684.

† The Muster Master would not enrol aliens. Their children would serve by allegiance of birth. At Norwich, in the Muster of 1621, the Dutch Company was 99 strong; J. van Berten was captain, Marcus Baelde lieutenant, and F. Duckets ensign bearer. Of the Walloon Company, 70 strong, Joel Sormeaux was captain, F. des Marets, lieutenant, and S. Caubre ensign.

called coleseed from which they press oil which serves well not only for the lamp but also to wash wool with."

The peat was burnt for manure, and cut into "turves" to serve as firewood and his nostrils were full of the smoke from the twitch-heaps. He ends his account thus :—

> In somma la terra è cosi facile da bruciâre che cadendo una scintilla di fuoco di candela s'accende e si stende sino à cinque passi di lunghezza e due piedi in profundo che pero il conestabile del luogo ordina di non fumar tabacco per le strade.

"In short the soil takes fire so easily that if a spark from a candle falls it kindles and spreads for five paces around and to the depth of two feet wherefore the constable of the town has ordered that no one shall smoke tobacco in the street."

You might put out the Dutchman's pipe; and if you left "the Minister" alone they would jog along. So it happened. Their hard work prospered during the Commonwealth, and at the Restoration, when the garb of the French ministers at Thorney, and their church discipline were unwelcome, the proclamation of Charles the Second soothed their apprehensions, and secured the strangers in the exercise of their privileges, till by the friendly aid of time their separate communion was voluntarily resigned, and their race absorbed in the English people.

> Charles the Sec[nd] by the grace of God &c.
>
> To all to whom these presents shall come greeting Whereas divers persons of ye French nation Walloon and others foreigners of the Reformed Protestant Religion who have been planted and long resided at Thorney in our Isle of Ely and County of Cambridge have humbly besought Us to grant unto them liberty of exercising their religion and discipline in ye church of Thorney in ye French tongue as they have hitherto practised Our will & pleasure is that the said Foreigners whether of the French Walloons or any other nation have and We do hereby accordingly give and grant unto them liberty and free exercise of Religion and discipline in ye church of Thorney aforesaid as it hath hitherto been practised by them wth power to make choice of Ministers and officers according to their discipline as hitherto they have done And Our further pleasure is that o[r] R[t]. Trusty and R[t]. Welbeloved cousin Willm Earle of Bedford owner of ye inheritance of Thorney and his heirs and ye Bishop of that diocese for ye time being have power from time to time of approving of ye Minister and officers so to be chosen And hereof all whom it may concern are to take notice and pay all due conformity to this Our pleasure.
>
> Given at Hampton Court, 13 August 1662.
>
> L. G.

911.—**Santoft Register** (652).—If the following paper should be the means of procuring information as to the whereabouts of this lost register, or further light as to its contents, a good purpose will be served. Of the antecedents of the congregations at Santoft and at Thorney little is known : and how it comes to pass that names known in South Lincolnshire in the sixteenth century should occur in both these French registers of a century later is a puzzle. We should welcome any communication that would have a tendency to throw light on an interesting phase of local history.

I am personally pleased to acknowledge the valuable services Mr. Peet is inclined to render in this connection. Under the auspices of the Huguenot Society of London it is hoped that both the registers will be printed; in the case of that of Thorney, if permission can be obtained, and of Santoft, if the register can be found.

Wryde, Thorney.   S. EGAR.

THE LOST REGISTER OF SANDTOFT CHAPEL,

containing Baptisms, Marriages, and Burials of the Dutch and Walloon Colony, settled at Sandtoft in Hatfield Chase,

Isle of Axholme.

An enquiry as to its fate and some suggestions concerning its probable destination.

The words employed by Hunter in his "South Yorkshire" (1828) in reference to the Sandtoft Register are very peculiar. He gives a list of the names of the foreign settlers "from the Register of the Chapel of Sandtoft, which was carefully kept, from 1641 to 1681, and is still in existence, or lately was so." There is something enigmatical about the above sentence. The words "*was carefully kept*" would imply that he had *seen* it, but the sentence which follows, "*and is still in existence, or lately was so,*" is capable of three interpretations. (1) That he had not seen it, very recently. (2) That he knew it was lost or destroyed, but for some reason, did not wish to publish the fact. (3) That he had never seen it. When he refers to the "Stovin Manuscript," he is careful to say that this interesting document had been in his possession, and that it was lent to him by the Rev. Dr. Stovin, then Rector of Rossington, the grandson of the author, Geo. Stovin, Esq., of Crowle, but in his reference to the Sandtoft Register he never once states that he had actually seen the volume, and it is significant that the list of names he enumerates are practically the same as those contained in the "Stovin MS."

Assuming, however, that it was in existence in 1828, and that Hunter had examined it, the question at once arises, in whose possession was it at that time? There is, of course, no doubt whatever that Stovin had it in his possession, but that was at least fifty years anterior to 1828. Stovin died an old man in 1780, and the latter years of his life were passed at Winterton, near Brigg, some distance from his old home at Crowle, in the Isle of Axholme. At Winterton he lived in a small cottage, and the probability is that his books would remain at Hirst Priory, Crowle, in the custody of his son, who on the retirement of his father to Winterton, took up his residence at Hirst Priory. In 1757 Stovin's son was elected Clerk to the Commissioners of Sewers of Hatfield Chase, and in 1771 Town Clerk of Doncaster—this latter office he held until 1778, that is, two years before the death of his father. He removed from Hirst Priory some time before this,—the date I am not able to fix,—to Rossington, where he built a house. It would appear that he again removed, to another residence, as he died at Sprotborough Hall, Rossington, in 1789. Some members of the Stovin family continued to reside at Hirst Priory. But to return to the year 1828. Stovin's grandson was then Vicar of Rossington, and we know he had the "Stovin Manuscript" in his possession. Had he also the Sandtoft Register? or was it amongst the books at Hirst Priory? Assuming that it was at Hirst Priory, it may give some clue if the successive occupiers of this charming residence can be identified.

In *1834* Allen, in his History of Lincolnshire, says "Two miles N. of Belton is Hirst Priory the seat of C. Stovin Esq."

In the Lincolnshire Directory for *1842* I find "Cornelius Hartshorn Stovin Esq. resides at Hirst Priory." (He died there in 1847).

After this date the Listers, who intermarried with the Stovins, appear on the scene. James Lister was a Landowner in the neighbourhood, and the patron of some Church livings.

1843. Rev. George Stovin Lister was Vicar of Luddington (a village near Hirst Priory).

1858. George Spofforth Lister, son of James Lister, of Ousefleet Hall, was the occupier of Hirst Priory.

1881. Mr. Bayley, in his "Ballieuls of Flanders," says "it (the Sandtoft Register) was believed to be traced to the possession of M^r. George Spofforth Lister, a gentleman residing at Hirst Priory, but the result of an application to him was that he could not find it."

The next year Hirst Priory was let to strangers. George Spofforth Lister, Esq., who is upwards of 90 years of age, now resides at Finningley Park, Bawtry.

If Hunter examined the Register at the same time that he made extracts from Stovin's Manuscript, it is not unlikely that the same fate awaited both the volumes. Stovin's MS. mysteriously disappeared, and was only discovered so recently as 1880, in the office of a Solicitor at Doncaster, much connected with the legal affairs of the Level of Hatfield Chase. From whence it came, or how long it had been lying there, could not be explained. The Register, being in French or Dutch, it may have been discarded and turned out as lumber; it appears quite certain that Hunter returned the "Stovin MS." Did he return the Sandtoft Register? Can any reader inform me if any descendants of Hunter are now living? I should gladly welcome any suggestion as to its probable hiding place. Three places suggest themselves.

(1) Buried amongst the books of some member of the family.
(2) In the parish chest at Rossington, or Luddington, or one of the neighbouring churches.
(3) In the office of one of the local Solicitors at Doncaster, Epworth, or Crowle.

There is, of course, the possibility that Hunter had the Register in his possession in 1828, that he never returned it to the person from whom he borrowed it, and that it is now in the possession of one of his descendants.

The "Stovin MS." is now (Aug. 1901) in the possession of Messrs. Loxley and Somerville, Solicitors, Doncaster, who act for the Corporation, which now represents the interest of the Participants in the Level of Hatfield Chase.

Mount Pleasant,   HENRY PEET, F.S.A.
Liverpool, Aug., 1901.

967.—Wanty Family of Thorney (925).—In our last number we gave a short notice of Mr. Peet's privately printed *Memorials of the Huguenot Family of de Vantier*. By the kindness of the author we are now enabled to give a page of the armorial bearings of some branches of the family. The different coats are so completely unlike, that in England we should feel inclined to question the fact that the families could have descended from one stock : but very possibly the rules of foreign heraldry are not the same as ours.

In tracing the careers of the members of one of the Huguenot families, Mr. Peet is naturally obliged to give some account of the reasons for leaving their native land ; and, accordingly, much of what he relates applies equally to members of others who for the same reasons felt compelled to emigrate to England in the 16th and 17th centuries. To those who live near the centres where these foreigners settled, and who are acquainted with some of the descendants of the original settlers, these details are of the greatest interest.

The French Church at Thorney was established in 1652. This was 33 years before the revocation of the Edict of Nantes, which caused a far greater number of the Huguenots to seek the hospitality of our shores, so that the first settlers at Thorney were driven to England in consequence of the persecution at the latter end of the 16th century.

We quote some passages describing the causes of the original coming.

There were two great immigrations of Huguenots from Flanders and France. The first commenced a few years immediately anterior to the Massacre on St. Bartholomew's Day (1572), and continued for many years, with varying flow, as the Persecution waxed and waned. It consisted partly of French and partly of Flemish Protestants—these latter were French-speaking Flemings or Walloons. The second, and numerically the greater immigration, occurred at the Revocation of the Edict of Nantes in 1685, and consisted almost entirely of French Huguenots. They found an asylum in this country, and settled in various places.

The French congregation at Thorney does not appear to have received any accession of members at this period. In the five years next after the Revocation not a single baptism appears in any family which was not settled at Thorney before that event.

The history of the Refugees in their settlements in England is intensely interesting, but the literature on the subject is at present confined to very narrow limits. The splendid work now being accomplished by the Huguenot Society of London in printing the Registers of the French Churches and other important documents long pigeon-holed at the Record Office, or buried amongst State Papers, will add materially to the sources of knowledge available for the student and genealogist. Holland and England constituted the principal asylum of the exiled Huguenots, especially those resident in the Northern Provinces of France. Holland in the first instance, and England in the next—many of the Refugees passing through one country on their way to the other. In Holland they naturally became adepts in the art of Embanking and Drainage, and as is well known, a certain section, when they came to England, rallied to the call of Vermuyden—the Dutch Engineer—in the great Drainage works he undertook in the Fens of Lincolnshire and the adjacent counties. The successful reclamation of the drowned lands was to a great extent due to the skilled labour and patient industry of the French and Walloon Colony, which for the greater part of a century made Thorney its home. In the course of time, not a few of the refugee community, cut off from their native land, married with their English neighbours, although at first the practice was discouraged. The names of these foreign strangers—anglicised and corrupted often past recognition—abound in every village and hamlet throughout the district, but the tongue of La Belle France has long since ceased to be heard in the Fens.

The old home of the de Vantiers is Le Pays de l'Alleud. This was situated in France, quite close to Belgium.

It was on the line of towns and villages between Armentières and Valenciennes, situated within a few miles of the present frontier of France and Belgium, and mostly within the province of French Flanders, then forming a part of the Spanish Netherlands, that the storm of persecution first fell.

It had the reputation of being one of the richest districts in Europe, renowned for its industry and thriving manufacture of linen and wool. The earliest members of the family who left the fatherland were Jaques Wantier, who in 1567 was sentenced to banishment in consequence of his religious zeal and active opposition to the cruelties of the Spaniards, and Jean Wantier and another Jaques, his brother, who were also sentenced to banishment in 1568. "The same sentence was passed upon Anna Wantier, the wife of Renault le Roy, for breaking images in various churches."

Maidstone and Canterbury were among the first places in England colonised by the Refugees. Numerous instances occur in the Registers of the French Church at Canterbury of baptisms and marriages of Wantiers between 1586 and 1628. As is well known, the crypt of Canterbury Cathedral was made over to the French settlers as a weaving factory; and the south aisle of the crypt was appropriated to their use as a place of worship: and to this day, Divine Service is still conducted there in the French language, although there is now no French-speaking community in the city.* Offices in the French Church were held by different members of the family. But after 1644 all such entries in the Registers and other books cease; so there was "evidently a dispersal of the family about this period."

By degrees some Wantiers seemed to have returned to Flanders. Descendants of the first exiles are found living at the old home at La Gorgue, but, as we might expect from the confiscation of their property, in much reduced circumstances. And once more, in the middle of the 17th century, persecution raged again, and the family, who now were always named de Vantier, were obliged to escape. "A few joined their relatives in England"; but most, in 1661, went to the Palatinate, where they stayed till driven away by the French in 1698, when they made their way to Denmark.

Some details which Mr. Peet has collected of this later emigration confirm the fact that the ancestral home of the family was at La Gorgue. Members can be clearly traced through the Palatinate to many places in Denmark and Germany, "where many of their descendants are now living."

It is to be noted that the colony of Huguenots at Thorney did not come to that place direct from abroad. They had first tried to establish themselves at the work at Hatfield Chase, in Yorkshire: but their presence there was resented, and they

* Canterbury Cathedral, in Bell's Series, p. 100.

were "molested by the peasantry." They accordingly made overtures to the Earl of Bedford to rent land on his Thorney estate, which they would drain and cultivate. With them there came some new arrivals from Flanders, as well as others who had already been living in Canterbury, London, and elsewhere in England. Mr. Peet divides the Thorney settlers into **three classes : (I) the trained drainers, who received wages for their work ; (II) the agriculturists, eager to avail themselves of the low rental at Thorney ; (III) the capitalists, who in some instances purchased land, and sometimes joined the body of the Adventurers.** The Wantys, and the Bailleuls (Bayleys) belonged to this last class. Among the purchasers of land were members of the families of Ris, La Pla, Le Cont, Prevost, Egar, and Melville.

✝

THE HUGUENOT PRAYER

A Collect to ask of God the assistance of His grace in the time of persecution

"O God, who art justly displeased with us, and with our brethren who are groaning under the weight of persecution. We beseech Thee, that it may please Thee to calm the tempest which overwhelms them. Pardon their unfaithfulness and their lukewarmness which arrests the course of Thy mercies towards them, and which exposes them to the saddest effects of the hatred of their enemies. Forgive them, O good God, and be not angry with them for ever. Do not look what justice would demand, see only that which asks Thy mercy. Defend Thy cause, deliver Thy people, and bless Thy heritage: remember Thy covenant and Thy promises made through Jesus Christ our Lord, that if Thou wilt not shorten the days of their calamities, and glorify Thy name in delivering them, O God, accomplish Thy work in their infirmities; increase their faith and strengthen their hope; kindle their love, and direct and sustain them by Thy spirit, so that considering they suffer for Thy cause, not only may they suffer with patience, but even may they glorify Thee in their tribulations: waiting for the reward which Thou hast promised them through Thy Son, who in union with the Holy Spirit, lives and reigns, one only God, blessed for ever. Amen."

OTHER FENLAND PUBLICATIONS BY THE SAME AUTHOR

A POCKET GUIDE TO THE FENS

FENLAND SAINTS, SHRINES AND CHURCHES

HEREWARD – The siege of the Isle of Ely involving the monasteries of Peterborough and Ely; also including De Gestis Herwardi Saxonis (The Adventures of Hereward the Saxon), in English

MINI STORIES FROM THE FENS

THORNEY'S MITRED ABBEY

A WALK AROUND THORNEY

FENLAND PLACES REVISITED

Obtainable from booksellers, cathedral bookshops and from the author, 28 St. Peter's Road, March, Cambs. PE15 9NA (Tel: (0354) 57286